A World of Work

in pictures

Pictures
to share

Joseph Edmondson, cotton weaver, poultry
breeder and show judge, Methodist lay
preacher, musician and violin maker.

**Pictures
to share**

First published in 2012 by
Pictures to Share Community Interest Company,
a UK based social enterprise that publishes
illustrated books for older people.

www.picturestoshare.co.uk

ISBN 978-0-9563818-3-5

Front Cover: Scene from a farm in Yorkshire 1980
                © John Downing / Hulton Archive / Getty Images
Front endpaper: Man painting wall © T-Immagini / istock photo
Title page: Tea in India 1940's
Back endpaper: UK Police women © Jenna Wagner / istock photo
Back cover: Detail from Chimney Sweep. Page 15
                Detail from Policewomen. Back endpaper
                Clock. From page 8

A World of Work
in pictures

Edited by Helen J Bate

The 1929 American stock market crash set off global economic shock waves.

UK unemployment rose to three million.

Bobby Shafto's gone to sea

Silver buckles on his knee,
He'll come back and marry me,
Bonny Bobby Shafto.

Bobby Shafto's bright and fair
Panning out his yellow hair;
He's my love for evermore,
Bonny Bobby Shafto.

Quotation: Bobby Shafto is a traditional 18th century English folk song.
Photograph: Fisherman at St Peter Port, Guernsey, UK.
© VisitBritain/Britain on View/Getty Images

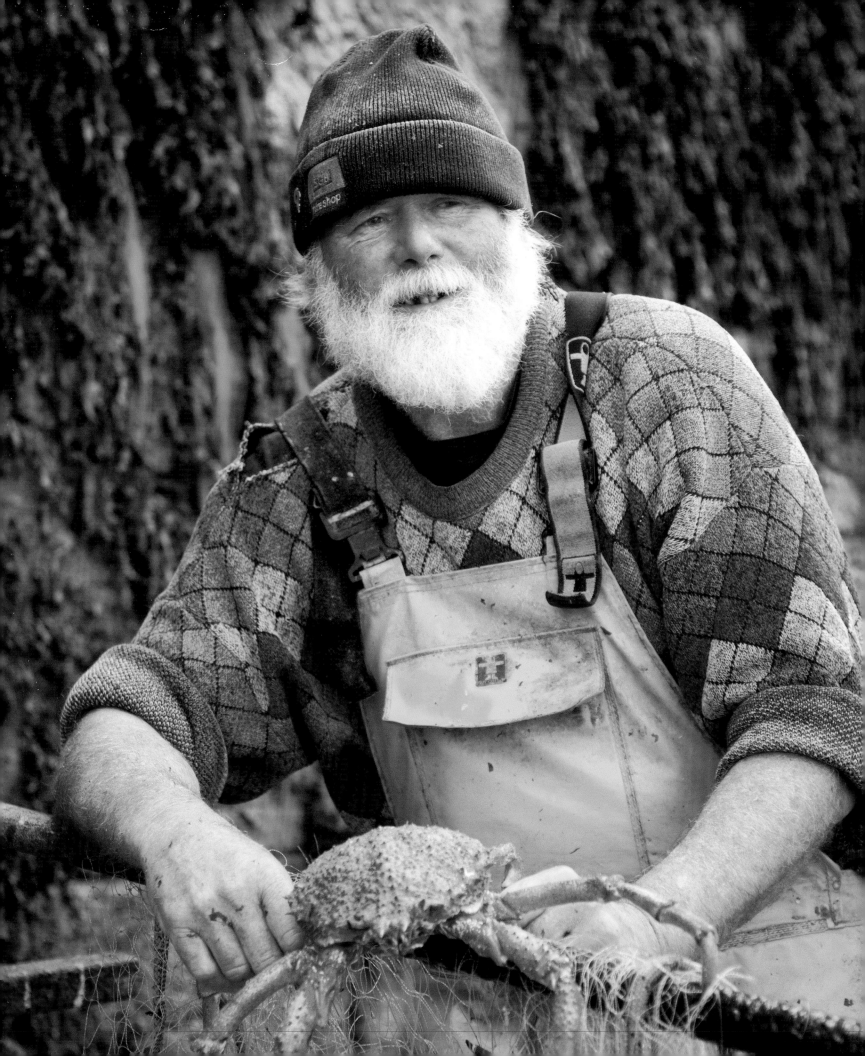

Working nine to five

what a way to make living

Barely getting by
it's all taking and no giving.

They just use your mind
and they never give you credit

It's enough to drive you crazy
if you let it.

Quotation: From song 'Nine to Five' by Dolly Parton
(1946 -) US singer songwriter

Main photograph: A Clerk at Lloyd's of London.
© Three Lions/Hulton Archive/Getty Images

Small photograph: © Nastco/istockphoto

I've been working so hard
you just wouldn't believe,

And I'm tired!

There's so little time
and so much to achieve,

And I'm tired!

Quotation: Extract from 'I've Been Working So Hard' by Sheldon Allan Silverstein (1932 - 1999) American poet, author and illustrator

Photographs: Mrs Thurtell, a cleaner employed by Boots the Chemist at work in London in 1953. © Bert Hardy/Picture Post/Hulton Archive/Getty Images

Small photograph: © klosfoto/istockphoto

The secret of life
is not to do what you like,
but to like what you do.

Courage
is the art
of being
the only
one who
knows
you're
scared
to death.

Quotation: Harold Wilson (1916 - 1995),
British Prime Minister in the 1960's and 1970's

Photographs: A chimney sweep climbing a chimney 1940
© Edwina Gnika/Keystone/Getty Images

Too many cooks spoil the broth

Quotation: Traditional proverb

Main photograph: Chefs in a large commercial kitchen.
© Art Montes De Oca/Photographer's Choice/Getty Images

Small photograph: © Simon Watson/The Image Bank/Getty Images

A Royal wedding 1934

The wedding cake made for the marriage
of the Duke of Kent and Princess Marina
of Greece was nine feet high
and weighed 800lbs.

A woman working at a comptometer

at the offices of Martin's Bank, Knightsbridge, London in 1961.

The Comptometer was the first commercial calculating machine.

An understanding heart is everything in a teacher.

One looks back with appreciation to the brilliant teachers,

but with gratitude to those who touched our human feeling.

Quotation: Carl Jung, Swiss psychologist (1875 - 1961)
Photograph: Girl and teacher. © LWA/Taxi/Getty Images

Any old iron,
Any old iron,
Any any any old iron?

You look neat
Talk about a treat,

You look dapper
from your napper to your feet.

Dressed in style, brand new tile,
And your father's old green tie on,

But I wouldn't give you tuppence
for your old watch chain;

Old iron, old iron?

Quotation: Words from 'Any Old Iron', a popular song
from 1911 by Charles Collins (1874 - 1926)

Photograph: A female dustman carries a tub full of old cans
back to her dustcart. Women in Ilford were the first to work
as dustwomen during WW2.
© Fred Ramage/Hulton Archive/Getty Images

Those who were
seen dancing
were thought to be insane
by those who
could not hear the music

Painting: Two Dancers on Stage 1874 by Edgar Degas.
Courtauld Institute and Galleries/Superstock/Getty Images

Quotation: Friedrich Wilhelm Nietzsche (1844-1900)
German philosopher and poet.

The wise man built his house upon the rock,

The wise man built his house upon the rock,
The wise man built his house upon the rock,
And the rain came tumbling down.

Oh, the rain came down
And the floods came up,

The rain came down
And the floods came up,

The rain came down
And the floods came up,

And the house on the rock stood firm.

Quotation: Children's hymn 1948 by Ann Omley

Main photograph: Bricklaying. © Haywood Magee
/HultonArchive/Getty Images

A stitch in time
saves nine.

Quotation: Traditional saying.

Main photograph: Leonard Barratt checks the measurements
of a customer being fitted with a bulletproof waistcoat.
© Harry Kerr/Hulton Archive/Getty Images

Small photograph. Sewing machine. © c-foto/istockphoto

There are only two kinds of freedom in the world;

the freedom of the rich and powerful, and the freedom of the artist who renounces possessions.

Quotation: Anais Nin US (French-born) author & diarist (1903 - 1977)

Painting: Felicien Rops (1833 - 1898) in his studio (oil on canvas)
by Paul Mathey (1844 - 1929) Chateau de Versailles, France
/The Bridgeman Art Library/Getty Images

Small photo: © Philartphace/istockphoto

In 1984, **striking miners** occupied the National Coal Board headquarters in London.

They were protesting against the arrest of union leader, Arthur Scargill.

Always laugh
when you can.
It is cheap medicine.

Our job as nurses

is to cushion the sorrow
and celebrate the joy

while we are
just doing our job.

Quotation: Christine Belle http://www.nursingschools.net/blog

Photograph: © Vecchio/Hulton Archive/Getty Images

...two hours
of pushin' broom
Buys an eight by twelve
four-bit room
I'm a man of means
by no means

King of the road.

Quotation: from King of the Road, song by Roger Miller
(1936-1992) American singer songwriter

Main photograph: A lorry driver for Baston Quarry,
Lincolnshire in his cab. © Needle/Hulton Archive/Getty Images

GRAVEL WORKS LTD

Baston Quarry Lincs

At length the stir of rural labour's still,

And Industry her care awhile forgoes;
When Winter comes in earnest to fulfil
His yearly task, at bleak November's close,
And stops the plough,
and hides the field in snows;

Quotation: From 'The Shepherds Calendar - November'
by John Clare, English poet (1793 - 1864)

Painting: And Dick the shepherd blows his nail, 1886 Edward Frederick
Brewtnall (1846 - 1902) The Bridgeman Art Library/Getty Images

I've got sixpence
Jolly, jolly sixpence,

I've got sixpence
to last me all my life.

I've got twopence to spend,
And twopence to lend,

And twopence to take
home to my wife...

poor wife.

Quotation: From 1940's folk song.

Main photograph: A young miner from Ellington Colliery, Northumberland, checks his pay packet
© Charles Hewitt/Hulton Archive/Getty Images

Small photograph: Silver sixpence. H Bate

Fred Smyth,
a sixty eight year old
worker with
the gas board,
shows off his
winning pools coupon.

Now he can retire
in luxury!

Pictures to share

Acknowledgements
Our thanks to the contributors who have allowed their imagery to be used for a reduced or no fee.

Thanks to our sponsors

ANDREWS CHARITABLE TRUST

Published by
Pictures to Share Community Interest Company
Tattenhall, Cheshire
www.picturestoshare.co.uk

Graphic design by Duncan Watts

Printed in England by
Langham Press, Station Road, Foxton
Cambridgeshire CB22 6SA

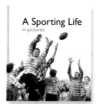

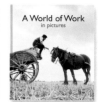

To see our other titles go to
www.picturestoshare.co.uk